Emily's New Friend

Emily Post

Emily's
New
Friend

by CINDY POST SENNING, Ed.D., and PEGGY POST
illustrated by STEVE BJÖRKMAN

Collins
An Imprint of HarperCollinsPublishers

Emily Post is a registered trademark of The Emily Post Institute, Inc.
Collins is an imprint of HarperCollins Publishers.

Emily's New Friend
Text copyright © 2010 by The Emily Post Institute, Inc.
Illustrations copyright © 2010 by Steve Björkman
All rights reserved. Manufactured in China.
No part of this book may be used or reproduced in any manner whatsoever without written permission except
in the case of brief quotations embodied in critical articles and reviews. For information address HarperCollins
Children's Books, a division of HarperCollins Publishers, 10 East 53rd Street, New York, NY 10022.
www.harpercollinschildrens.com

Library of Congress Cataloging-in-Publication Data
Senning, Cindy Post.
    Emily's new friend / by Cindy Post Senning and Peggy Post ; illustrated by Steve Björkman. — 1st ed.
       p.   cm.
    Summary: Emily and a new neighbor become friends by treating each other with generosity, kindness,
and good manners. Includes a note for parents on the importance of teaching principles of etiquette at home.
    ISBN 978-0-06-111706-0 (trade bdg.) — ISBN 978-0-06-111707-7 (lib. bdg.)
    [1. Friendship—Fiction. 2. Conduct of life—Fiction. 3. Etiquette—Fiction. 4. Neighbors—
Fiction.] I. Post, Peggy. II. Björkman, Steve, ill. III. Title.
PZ7.S476En 2010   2009011767
[E]—dc22   CIP
                                                            AC

Typography by Jeanne L. Hogle
10 11 12 13 14 SCP 10 9 8 7 6 5 4 3 2 1
❖
First Edition

We dedicate this to the friends we've made over the years.
You mean the world to us!
There is nothing better than friendship.
—C.P.S. and P.P.

For Kristi's friends Jessica and Cody
—S.B.

Today, Emily is lonely.
Her mom is busy.
Her dad is busy.
Even Nutmeg is busy.
She wishes a kid her age
lived in the neighborhood.

Today Ethan is lonely.
He is also a little scared.
Ethan is moving to a new town.
He misses his friends. He wonders
if he will make new ones.

How do you meet someone new?
All it takes is a little courage, a big smile,
and some help from Mom or Dad!

Hi, my name is Emily.
I brought you some cookies.
Welcome to our street!

Emily gives Ethan a big welcome.
She brings a gift.
She introduces herself and smiles.

It is easy to start
a new friendship.
Emily offers to help.

She shows Ethan
around.

Ethan is relieved.
He doesn't feel as
lonely anymore.

Neither does Emily.

Emily invites Ethan over to play.

She is considerate.
She asks Ethan what
he wants to do.

She shares her markers . . .

and offers a special snack.

Ethan shows he can be a
good friend, too!

He invites Emily to his house
and lets her pick the game.

He shows her his favorite
toys . . .

. . . and gives her a playful surprise! They both like to laugh!

Emily and Ethan discover they like many of the same things.

Emily likes to swim. So does Ethan!

Ethan's favorite color is yellow. Emily loves yellow, too.

They both like books, and they read out loud to each other.

When it is time to go home, Ethan and Emily always help each other clean up.

And at the end of a playdate, they both know what to say to each other: THANK YOU!!!!

Soon, Emily and Ethan are
together all the time.
They ride the bus together.

They play at the park

They help each
other learn new
things.

They cheer each other on.
They don't brag or tease.
They are not mean or bossy.

Emily knocks on the door.

Ethan wipes his feet on the mat.

Emily and Ethan always show *respect* for each other.

You know, respect just means showing people you care about them—even if they look different from you, talk differently, or aren't your best friend.

They are always *considerate* of each other.

They always tell each other the positive *truth*!

This is why Ethan and Emily
are the very best of friends.

If you treat others with respect
and consideration and honesty,
you can be a best friend too!

Dear Parents,

One of the great challenges of childhood is learning to make and keep good friends. Whether they are gregarious and outgoing or quiet and shy, few children are naturally blessed with the skills they need for this important social activity. Social skills—including manners—are learned, just like reading and math. There are specific skills that children use as they make and keep friends. The mastery of these skills will enable them to deal more effectively and easily in a variety of situations. What you teach your children today will someday translate into gracious behavior and meaningful relationships in all areas of their lives.

Children need to learn to:

- Use polite behavior. Good manners matter with everyone: their peers, their family, and other adults in their lives.
- Share and take turns.
- Communicate.
- Cooperate.
- Understand social cues—verbal and nonverbal signals people use to communicate their feelings and wishes.

But there is more to making friends than basic skills or manners. The fundamental principles of etiquette—consideration, respect, and honesty—are a critical part of the equation. While they learn to use these basic skills on the playground and in the classroom, children essentially learn the principles at home. Children who see their parents as kind, considerate, respectful, and honest people will become kind, considerate, respectful, and honest themselves. Once they combine these attributes with the basic skills, they have the ability to make and nurture friendships throughout their lives. What an amazing gift to give your child!

With best wishes for you and your children,
Cindy and Peggy